D0118935

MONEY MATTERS

Counting
Money

by Mari Schuh

BLASTOFF!
READERS
2

BELLWETHER MEDIA · MINNEAPOLIS, MN

Note to Librarians, Teachers, and Parents:

Blastoff! Readers are carefully developed by literacy experts and combine standards-based content with developmentally appropriate text.

Level 1 provides the most support through repetition of high-frequency words, light text, predictable sentence patterns, and strong visual support.

Level 2 offers early readers a bit more challenge through varied simple sentences, increased text load, and less repetition of high-frequency words.

Level 3 advances early-fluent readers toward fluency through increased text and concept load, less reliance on visuals, longer sentences, and more literary language.

Level 4 builds reading stamina by providing more text per page, increased use of punctuation, greater variation in sentence patterns, and increasingly challenging vocabulary.

Level 5 encourages children to move from "learning to read" to "reading to learn" by providing even more text, varied writing styles, and less familiar topics.

Whichever book is right for your reader, Blastoff! Readers are the perfect books to build confidence and encourage a love of reading that will last a lifetime!

This edition first published in 2016 by Bellwether Media, Inc.

No part of this publication may be reproduced in whole or in part without written permission of the publisher. For information regarding permission, write to Bellwether Media, Inc., Attention: Permissions Department, 5357 Penn Avenue South, Minneapolis, MN 55419.

Library of Congress Cataloging-in-Publication Data

Schuh, Mari C., 1975-
Counting Money / by Mari Schuh.
    pages cm. – (Blastoff! Readers: Money Matters)
  Summary: "Relevant images match informative text in this introduction to counting money. Intended for students in kindergarten through third grade"– Provided by publisher.
  Audience: Ages 5-8
  Audience: K to grade 3
  Includes bibliographical references and index.
   ISBN 978-1-62617-245-6 (hardcover: alk. paper)
  1. Counting–Juvenile literature. 2. Money–Juvenile literature. I. Title.
  QA113.S3888184 2016
  332.4–dc23
                        2015004207

Printed in the United States of America, North Mankato, MN.

Table of Contents

It is fun to count money. Many small **coins** can add up to big **bills**!

= actual size

This reddish brown
coin is a **penny**.
It is **worth** 1 **cent**.

A penny is the smallest amount of money in the United States.

A **nickel** equals 5 pennies.
A **dime** equals 10 pennies.

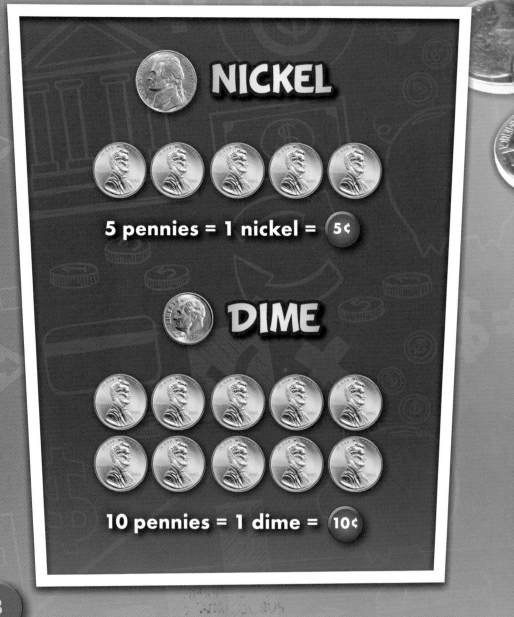

NICKEL

5 pennies = 1 nickel = 5¢

DIME

10 pennies = 1 dime = 10¢

= actual size = actual size

Both coins are silver in color.
The nickel is larger in size.

This even bigger silver-colored coin is a **quarter**. It equals 25 pennies. It also equals 5 nickels.

= actual size

QUARTER

25 pennies = 1 quarter = 25¢

5 nickels = 1 quarter = 25¢

Coins That Equal a $1 Bill

Many coins can add up to $1. That is the worth of the smallest U.S. bill.

ONE-DOLLAR BILL

100 pennies = $1

A one-dollar bill equals
100 pennies.

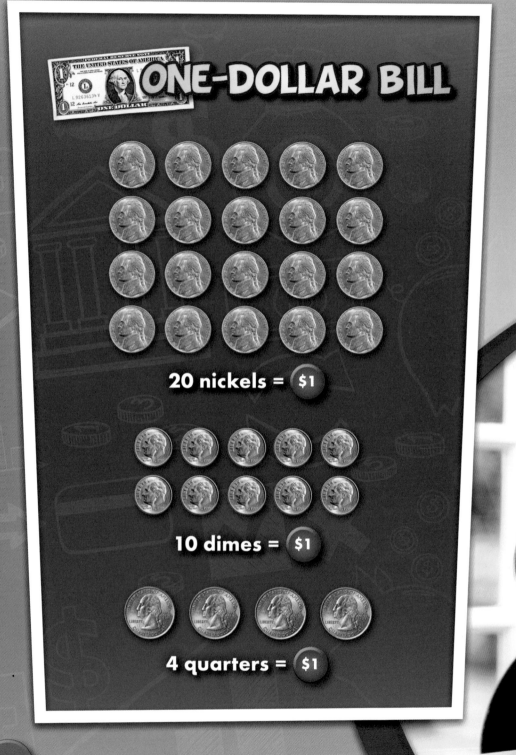

ONE-DOLLAR BILL

20 nickels = $1

10 dimes = $1

4 quarters = $1

A one-dollar bill also equals 20 nickels or 10 dimes. Only 4 quarters are needed to make one dollar.

Bills That Equal a $100 Bill

A hundred-dollar bill is the biggest U.S. bill. It is worth $100.

It equals 100 one-dollar bills.
It also equals 10 ten-dollar bills.

HUNDRED-DOLLAR BILL

5 twenty-dollar bills = $100

2 fifty-dollar bills = $100

18

= actual size

A hundred-dollar bill is worth
5 twenty-dollar bills. It is also
worth just 2 fifty-dollar bills!

Adding It All Up

25¢ + 25¢ = 50¢

50¢ + 50¢ = $1.00

10¢ + 10¢ = 20¢

People should count their money.
Then they will know how much
they can spend and save!

Glossary

bills—paper money

cent—the smallest amount of U.S. money;
a penny is worth 1 cent.

coins—round pieces of money that are
made of metal

dime—a coin worth 10 cents

nickel—a coin worth 5 cents

penny—a coin worth 1 cent

quarter—a coin worth 25 cents

worth—having a certain value

To Learn More

AT THE LIBRARY

Alaina, Maria. *Counting Money*. North Mankato, Minn.: Capstone Press, 2012.

Duke, Shirley Smith. *Money Counts*. Vero Beach, Fla.: Rourke, 2013.

Heo, Bridget. *Counting Change*. Mankato, Minn.: Amicus Illustrated, 2015.

ON THE WEB

Learning more about counting money is as easy as 1, 2, 3.

1. Go to www.factsurfer.com.

2. Enter "counting money" into the search box.

3. Click the "Surf" button and you will see a list of related web sites.

With factsurfer.com, finding more information is just a click away.

Index

The images in this book are reproduced through the courtesy of: cowardlion, cover, p. 20 (boy); dibrova, cover, p. 20 (left bills); martan, cover, p. 20 (dollar signs); Christos Georghiou, cover, p. 20 (equal sign, plus sign); Robyn Mackenzie, cover, p. 20 (dollar coin, top right bills, pennies); rsooll, cover (dimes), pp. 8, 9, 14 (nickel, dime), p. 11 (nickel); Dan Kosmayer, cover, p. 20 (calculator); David Brimm, cover, back cover (bottom coins); John Brueske, p. 4; JGI/ Jamie Grill/ Corbis, pp. 4-5, 20-21; Sascha Burkard, pp. 6, 8, 11, 13 (penny); S. M. Beagle, pp. 6-7; HodagMedia, pp. 8-9 (large dimes); Asaf Eliason, pp. 10, 11, 14 (quarter); PhotoInc, pp. 10-11; Michael A. Keller/ Corbis, p. 12; nimon, pp. 13, 14, 19 (one-dollar bill), p. 17 (one-dollar bills); Adie Bush/ Corbis, pp. 14-15; RUSS ROHDE/ Corbis, pp. 16-17; Andrey Lobachev, p. 17 (hundred-dollar bill); Robynrg, p. 17 (ten-dollar bills), p. 19 (ten-dollar bill); Karen Roach, pp. 18, 19 (twenty-dollar bills); indigolotos, pp. 18, 19 (fifty-dollar bills); sirikorn thamniyom, p. 19 (hundred-dollar bill).